SIMONE BILES

GYMNASTICS LEGEND

BY CHRÖS McDOUGALL

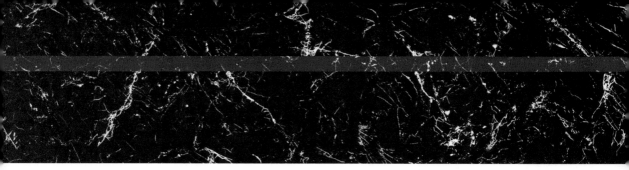

Book design by Jake Nordby
Cover design by Jake Nordby

Photographs ©: Ulrik Pedersen/Cal Sport Media/ZUMA Wire/AP Images, cover, 1; Jamie Squire/Getty Images Sport/Getty Images, 4, 7; Dean Mouhtaropoulos/Getty Images Sport/ Getty Images, 8, 13; Jared Wickerham/Getty Images Sport/Getty Images, 11; Lintao Zhang/ Getty Images Sport/Getty Images, 14; Elsa/Getty Images Sport/Getty Images, 17; Owen Humphreys/PA Wire/AP Images, 18, 30; Laurence Griffiths/Getty Images Sport/Getty Images, 20–21, 26; Daniel Zuchnik/WireImage/Getty Images, 22; Francois Nel/Getty Images Sport/ Getty Images, 24; Red Line Editorial, 29

Press Box Books, an imprint of Press Room Editions.

ISBN
978-1-63494-784-8 (library bound)
978-1-63494-804-3 (paperback)
978-1-63494-843-2 (epub)
978-1-63494-824-1 (hosted ebook)

Library of Congress Control Number: 2023909028

Distributed by North Star Editions, Inc.
2297 Waters Drive
Mendota Heights, MN 55120
www.northstareditions.com

Printed in the United States of America
012024

About the Author
Chrös McDougall is a sportswriter, editor, and author. He covered Simone Biles from her US Championships debut in 2013 through the 2021 Olympics in Tokyo, Japan.

TABLE OF CONTENTS

1 UNSTOPPABLE

The crowd in Kansas City, Missouri, quieted to a hush. Anytime Simone Biles performed on the floor exercise, it was a showstopper. But this night, at the 2019 US Gymnastics Championships, was special.

The 22-year-old Biles had dominated the sport for years. At the 2016 Olympics, she won four gold medals and a bronze. Then, after a break from the sport, she returned in 2018 and didn't miss a beat. At that year's World Championships, she

Simone Biles poses during her floor routine at the 2019 US Gymnastics Championships.

won four gold medals and six overall. What more could she possibly do in the sport? The fans in Kansas City were about to find out.

As the music started, Biles danced her way to the corner. Then, at the sound of a bell, she spun around and began sprinting toward the opposite corner. Showing near-perfect form, she performed a roundoff and then a back handspring. Using the power from those skills, she pushed off the floor with both feet and rose 10 feet (3 m) into the air. As she did, Biles spun three times to her left while flipping backward twice. Landing with the smallest of hops, Biles smiled brightly. The once-quiet crowd roared. Biles quickly carried on with the rest of her routine.

Gymnasts are always trying to push the limits of what's possible. Biles had already done

According to the US coach, the "triple-double" was the most difficult skill imaginable in women's floor exercise.

that numerous times in her career. Now she did it again. On this night, Biles became the first woman to land the "triple-double" on floor exercise. The world's greatest gymnast was only getting better.

2 RISING UP

Simone Biles was born on March 14, 1997, in Columbus, Ohio. However, she didn't stay there long. Her mom struggled with drugs and alcohol, and her dad wasn't part of her life. When Simone was around two years old, she and her three siblings entered foster care. Eventually their grandpa, Ron Biles, and his wife, Nellie, took them into their home in Spring, Texas. When Simone was six, they adopted her and her younger sister,

Simone Biles competes on vault at the 2013 World Championships.

Adria. Another family member adopted their older siblings.

That same year, Simone's day-care class took a field trip to a local gymnastics center. A coach there named Aimee Boorman noticed Simone right away. The young gymnast showed great control as she leaped through the air. "She was absolutely fearless," Boorman said. She suggested Simone sign up for classes. Boorman eventually became Simone's coach.

The sport came naturally to Simone. She could watch an older girl perform a difficult skill, then copy it. This helped her climb to higher and higher levels.

GIVING BACK

Through gymnastics and endorsements, Simone Biles has earned millions of dollars. She never forgot the hard times growing up, however. Biles regularly works with organizations that support kids in foster care. "Foster kids will always have a special piece of my heart," she said.

Aimee Boorman (right) coached Simone for 11 years.

But Simone wasn't perfect. Sometimes she struggled to control her power. Her technique needed to be improved as well.

Before starting high school, Simone decided to start homeschooling. This allowed her to train a lot more for gymnastics. And all that training soon began to pay off in competitions. By then, Simone was competing at the junior elite level. At the 2012 US Championships, she earned a win on vault and finished third in the all-around. Though her results didn't necessarily stand out, Simone's abilities were turning heads in the gymnastics community.

The next year, Simone moved up to the senior elite level. It is the highest level in the sport. But Simone got off to a disastrous start. Her first competition was the 2013 US Classic. After Simone fell on two events and nearly fell on another, Boorman pulled her from the competition. "I could tell that her mind wasn't where it needed to be," Boorman said.

Simone began meeting with a sports psychologist. Coaches gave her pep talks. By the time she arrived at the US Championships the next month, she was feeling confident. With her high-flying skills and boundless energy,

Simone (middle) poses with her all-around gold medal at the 2013 World Championships.

Simone beat out two Olympians to win the all-around title. A few weeks later, she did even better. At the World Championships in Belgium, she won the all-around and floor exercise. Still only 16 years old, Simone had a bright future ahead of her.

3 GOLDEN

Simone Biles came back in 2014 and did it all again. After winning another US title, she was brilliant at the World Championships. She came home from the event in China with four world titles, including another in the all-around. By then, her abilities were impossible to ignore. Mary Lou Retton was the first US gymnast to win an individual Olympic gold medal. She said Biles "may be the most talented gymnast I've ever seen in my life."

Biles competes in the floor exercise during the 2014 World Championships.

In 2015, Biles became the first woman to win three consecutive all-around world titles. Despite making some mistakes at the meet in Scotland, Biles won with her biggest margin of victory yet. That's because her routines were so difficult. Since withdrawing from the 2013 US Classic, Biles had won every all-around she entered. Most of those wins weren't even close. Her thrilling, high-energy gymnastics and seemingly boundless joy made her extremely popular.

Her dominance set sky-high expectations for Biles going into the 2016 Olympics in Rio de Janeiro, Brazil. There is no greater stage in gymnastics. If Biles was nervous, it didn't show during the qualifying session. Two days later, Biles was the lone US gymnast to compete in all four events in the team final. She opened

Biles flips on the balance beam in the all-around final at the 2016 Olympics.

with the ultra-difficult Amanar vault. Rising high into the air, twisting 2.5 times, and then landing without seeing the mat, Biles scored 15.933. No one posted a higher score all day. Biles then went on to earn the highest scores on balance beam and floor exercise, too. Led by her

Biles smiles with her team Olympic gold medal in 2016.

unflappable performance, the US women easily won the gold medal.

Biles's biggest individual test was next: the all-around. Once again, it was not close.

Ending on her best event, floor exercise, Biles seemed to float effortlessly through the air in her tumbling passes. After her final pose, Biles looked toward the sky and smiled. It was another gold-medal performance.

Biles also qualified for three individual event finals. A mistake while performing a somersault on balance beam was her only blemish. Biles won a bronze medal on that event, to go with gold medals on vault and floor. She became only the fifth female gymnast to win four gold medals in a single Olympics. On the biggest stage, she had shown again that she was the best in the world.

BLACK GYMNASTS

Simone Biles became the second Black gymnast to win an individual Olympic gold medal. Her US teammate Gabby Douglas had been the first in 2012. Two other Americans, Dominique Dawes and Betty Okino, became the first Black gymnasts to win Olympic medals in 1992.

ONE-OF-A-KIND SKILLS

Though standing just 4-foot-8 (142 cm), Simone Biles is incredibly powerful. On floor exercise, she can begin tumbling after just a few steps. This allows her to pack bigger skills into each pass. Massive dismounts on balance beam set her apart. And she seems to float through the air off the vault.

Power alone can't make great routines, though. From a young age, Biles was able to quickly learn new skills. By her teenage years, she had developed elite technique and body control. She was also incredibly consistent. Most top gymnasts stand out on one or two events. Biles became world-class on all four and nearly unbeatable on floor and vault.

In the gymnastics code, Biles has four skills named after her. One is on vault, one is on balance beam, and two are on floor. The skills are named *Biles* because she was the first to perform them at a major international competition.

Biles flies high in the air during a floor routine at the World Championships in 2019.

4 THE GREATEST

Simone Biles took some time away from gymnastics after the 2016 Olympics. She needed to relax. However, she also needed to heal. After the Olympics, it was revealed that a former team doctor had sexually abused more than 100 athletes. In early 2018, Biles shared that she was one of the victims.

The trauma deeply affected Biles. She said the US team had "failed" the gymnasts. This made it hard to compete for the team. But by 2018, she returned

During her time off after the Olympics, Biles released an autobiography titled *Courage to Soar.*

Biles's historic performance at the 2018 World Championships came after she spent the night before the competition in the hospital dealing with pain from a kidney stone.

to the sport. Despite her time off, she came back better than ever. At that year's US Championships, she swept all the gold medals. No one had done that since 1994. Then she won four gold and six total medals at the World

Championships. No woman had won a medal in all the individual events since 1987.

Biles extended her winning streak with a fifth all-around world title in 2019. She also won her fifth floor exercise world title. That gave her 19 world titles and 25 world championships medals. No gymnast, man or woman, had more.

Her second showing on the world's biggest stage had to wait, however. The 2020 Olympics in Tokyo, Japan, were postponed due to the COVID-19 pandemic. They took place in 2021 instead. But Biles was still ready. She won the all-around at the US Championships and the Olympic Trials. Then she got off to a good start in Tokyo, qualifying for every individual final.

Not all was going well, though. Biles arrived in Tokyo feeling great pressure. Her routines in qualifying hadn't been as sharp as usual.

Biles cheers on her teammates during the team final at the Olympics in 2021.

Then, in the team final, she experienced the "twisties." This is what a gymnast calls it when her mind and body aren't working together.

Fearing an injury and afraid of harming her team by competing poorly, Biles withdrew. She didn't feel ready again until the last day of competition. Performing a balance beam routine with no twists, she won a bronze medal.

It wasn't the Olympics that Biles had imagined. Many people misunderstood why she had withdrawn. Some criticized her for it. Others praised Biles for putting her well-being first. In the end, she said she was proud of her performance. It was another part of the legacy for the world's most decorated gymnast.

SPEAKING UP

After the 2016 Olympics, Simone Biles became more outspoken. She decried racism and abuse within the sport. Then her openness about mental health during the 2020 Olympics raised awareness about that issue. "I am really proud of her," fellow US gymnast Sam Mikulak said. She showed fans "that we're not just athletes," he added. "We're human beings."

TIMELINE

1. **Columbus, Ohio (March 14, 1997)**
   Simone Biles is born.

2. **Spring, Texas (2003)**
   After being adopted by her grandpa and his wife, Simone begins gymnastics lessons in her new hometown.

3. **Hartford, Connecticut (August 17, 2013)**
   Biles wins her first US title, beginning a winning streak in the all-around that continues to the Olympics in 2021.

4. **Glasgow, Scotland (October 23–November 1, 2015)**
   Biles wins four gold medals at the World Championships.

5. **Rio de Janeiro, Brazil (August 5–21, 2016)**
   Biles wins gold medals in the team, all-around, floor exercise, and vault in addition to a bronze medal on balance beam at the Olympics.

6. **Doha, Qatar (October 25–November 3, 2018)**
   Biles becomes the first woman to medal in all six events at the World Championships since 1987.

7. **Kansas City, Missouri (August 9, 2019)**
   At the US Championships, Biles becomes the first woman to successfully perform the "triple-double" on floor exercise.

8. **Tokyo, Japan (July 25–August 3, 2021)**
   Biles withdraws from four event finals at the Olympics for health reasons but still wins a silver medal in the team event and a bronze medal on balance beam.

MAP

N

Birth date: March 14, 1997

Birthplace: Columbus, Ohio

Size: 4-foot-8 (142 cm)

Olympic Games: 2016 (Rio de Janeiro, Brazil), 2021 (Tokyo, Japan)

Olympic medals: 4 gold, 1 silver, 2 bronze

World Championships: 2013 (Antwerp, Belgium), 2014 (Nanning, China), 2015 (Glasgow, Scotland), 2018 (Doha, Qatar), 2019 (Stuttgart, Germany)

World Championships medals: 19 gold, 3 silver, 3 bronze

Major awards: Associated Press Female Athlete of the Year (2016, 2019), Laureus World Sportswoman of the Year (2016, 2018), Presidential Medal of Freedom (2022)

Accurate through September 2023.

GLOSSARY

adopted
Legally became the parents of a child who had other birth parents.

all-around
The combination of every gymnastics event. The women's all-around includes balance beam, floor exercise, uneven bars, and vault.

code
A system of rules and guidelines. The gymnastics code of points includes the values for each skill.

dismount
When a gymnast leaves the apparatus at the end of a routine.

endorsements
Payments to someone to use and promote companies' products.

foster care
A system in which a temporary caregiver provides shelter to children who are unable to live with their families.

sports psychologist
A professional who studies the human mind and works with athletes to improve their performance.

trauma
A strong emotional response to a distressing event.

tumbling
Acrobatic moves including handsprings and somersaults. A series of these moves is called a tumbling pass.

TO LEARN MORE

Books

Hewson, Anthony K. *Simone Biles*. Minneapolis: Abdo Publishing, 2022.

Lawrence, Blythe. *Behind the Scenes Gymnastics*. Minneapolis: Lerner Publications, 2020.

Lawrence, Blythe. *Trailblazing Women in Gymnastics*. Chicago: Norwood House Press, 2023.

More Information

To learn more about Simone Biles, go to **pressboxbooks.com/AllAccess**.

These links are routinely monitored and updated to provide the most current information available.

INDEX